This Book Belon_____

No Chomping baby dino: A "no biting" book for toddlers
Copywrite©2023 Myspeechpals. All rights reserved. No portion of this book may be reproduced in any form without permission from the publisher, except as permitted by U.S. copyright law.

Once upon a time,
in a house near a swamp,

lived little Danny Dino who had the very best CHOMP!

He would CHOMP on his snacks the whole weekend,

but what he loved most of all was 'Hide-and-Seek' with his friends.

When it was his turn to hide, he'd turn and run with a STOMP!

"Ouch! Oh no, Danny Dino!
I don't like your
CHOMP CHOMPS!"

Danny Dino was so sad, and went home feeling blue.

So Danny practiced his words for the rest of the week,

YAY! I'm Excited!
YAY!
I'm Excited!
YAY!
YAY!
I'm Excited!
LET'S GO!
I'm Excited!
YAY!

until at last it was time to play 'Hide-and-Go-Seek'.

"Oh No, Danny Dino!
Your CHOMPS made me cry.
We don't want you to play.
No, we won't even try."

But his friends spoke to Suzie in her firm, grumpy stance, and they decided to give Danny one final chance.

Suzie counted past four, and
Danny ran with a STOMP.
But as he ran, he forgot,
and he wanted to CHOMP!

1 2 3 4

They all had a good laugh. "What a silly way to play!"

And now he plays
'Hide-and-Seek'
with his friends everyday.

Thank you for supporting small businesses.

Here are some additional titles you may enjoy!

Early Childhood Intervention Specialist
Speech and Language Therapist
-B. Daugherty CCC SLP

Made in the USA
Middletown, DE
22 September 2023

39081038R00015